How
She
Bleeds

Cover Design: TreManda Pewett
Editor: Carla DuPont Huger
Illustration: TreManda Pewett

ISBN 13: 978-0-9862556-4-9
ISBN 10: 0-9862556-4-5

Jeanius Publishing LLC
430 Lee Blvd
Lehigh Acres, FL 33936
For more information, please visit:
Jeaniuspublishing.com

How
She
Bleeds

Porsha M. Allen

Dedication

Someone once asked me why I write. The truth is, writing is the only thing that makes me feel like I am 'enough.' I can only hope that through this book, you learn what it means to acknowledge, accept, and heal yourself from the inside out. Some of these poems were painful to write, and for a while I struggled with whether or not I should reveal such pain and secrets. I wrote this book for both of us. I am humbled that you chose to embark on this journey with me. It is my prayer that you find healing, while knowing that you are not alone. This book was my healing process; I dedicate it to you.

With Love,
Porsha M. Allen

Acknowledgements

To my family and friends:
Thank you for all of your love, support, and words of
encouragement; for crying with me, laughing with me, and
inspiring me to give birth to this book. Thank you for your
wise words and your unfailing and unwavering love for me.

Table of Contents

OPEN WOUNDS

I didn't believe you when you said you were leaving;
evidence of your betrayal grew inside her stomach.
She had your child - a girl.
Did you name her after your guilt, forgetting that I
had a stomach filled with pain and regret?

- The breaking

Monsters Like You

Daddy,

he had claws like yours, long, thick,

used for digging,

for destroying,

for picking away at the bones of the dead.

He came,

touched the parts of me

that were reserved for my husband on our wedding

night,

then scurried into the darkness of the hallway.

And ever since that day,

I've always been afraid of monsters,

afraid that men would lurk, or would

crawl.

I don't remember having tea parties and playing dress

up. Instead, I spent years trying to unclothe myself of

the resentment you caused.

I haven't figured out how I am to be treated, only

how my body is parted.

You poisoned my perception.

The sound of my mother's cracked ribs,

my brother's jaw breaking, all sound a lot like
wedding vows;
the blood on my grandmother's nightgown,
and your boot pressed in my sister's side, make as
beautiful family portraits.

You were the first man to ever make me cry,
to ever place his hands around my neck,
to ever expose me to the color of blood,
or cracked glass,
or the smell of death.
You were the first man to ever break my heart
and the first to never apologize for it.

I coughed up your bones
last night, and dreamed
someone had placed you
next to me. This is how
we were supposed to die -
together, plucking weeds from
one another's corpse.

- passing

They peel back the layers of her skin.
Honey drips from every part of her being,
while the men look for mason jars.
She is captured and sucked to the bone.
Each one places his hand inside her,
inhaling, and savoring her sweetness.
Each one scrapes the last of her from their mason
jars, their fingers becoming more sticky than before.
Their bellies still howl for her as they look
to be filled to the brim.
There are still some parts of her that are left dripping,
but only from the corners of their mouths.

Forgive me
for not knowing
how to be anything
more than broken.

- still learning

Journal entry

September 12, 2015

I never liked funerals.

Too many people, with some shedding the kind of tears you know aren't real.

I was eight when my great-grandmother passed away. She raised my sister and I.

 I remember when the firefighters pulled her body out of her own house; the way she slumped over when my mother tried to help her to the bathroom. That's all I could think about during the funeral, that and windows. I tried to break one when I saw the ambulance take her away. I never liked ruffle socks either, but Grandma made my sister and I wear them to church every Sunday. That day though, as I looked down at my feet, and my polished, black patent leather shoes, I didn't mind them all that much. I wore a white dress with a red ribbon on the front that I couldn't stop messing with. I thought about the pink dress that my great-grandmother wanted me to wear Sundays before. Grandma always tried to make me wear it, though I never did. I looked at her closed eyes and neatly folded hands from my seat. I wanted to shake her, ask her to read the book of Genesis to

me again, and offer to get her a drink of water before
bed. But I couldn't.

Today, I wish I had worn the pink dress with the
ruffle socks to match.

The white one always made me itch.

Violation

He undressed her mind with his enticing
manipulation,
stroked her cheek with the same hand he used to
wrap around her throat,
stretched her self-esteem until it disintegrated into the
ashes
used to dress those beautiful coffins,
and fertilized her egg with his cement.
She vandalized the walls with the redness from her
veins,
and silently waited for death's arrival
-but it never came.

I knew I was in danger
when I could not remember
my own name.
I was his,
the only thing I knew to
answer to.

- What is done for love

Nightfall

When she whispers his name,
the picture of them on the night stand moves.
He is smiling with his arm around her shoulder,
and her right hand is placed gently on his chest.
She pours liquor into a shot glass
and watches as the ice disappears,
dissolving the same way he did,
the same way her body did
when it came to know his hands.

There is a brown leather notebook
dipped in bitter red wine and cigarette ash
underneath her bed.
She looks inside to see every poem,
half written about him,
the first starting from the day that he left.

She turns on James Brown and listens as his voice
drifts along with the night fog, stretching itself like a
blanket around her bare body. Tears drip like acid
down her cheeks giving them all a name, room to
breathe,
to exist.

She closes her eyes and imagines their spirits making
love to the sound of the wind.
It has been two months and she is still waiting for
him.
She can tell by the way of the moon that it has been
waiting for him too,
so that it may return back to its fullness.

"What are you going to say to her when she gets here?" asked my friend, Amber, as she dipped her chocolate chip cookie into almond milk. "I don't know," I said. As I changed my sheets that smelled of old happiness and coffee, I looked around my room and wondered if I should tell her not to come.

We did everything together. The first time we met, I was in the third grade and two girls in my class had been picking on me about my hair. I had just moved in with my mother and older siblings, and I did not fit in or even cared to. She sat with me at a round table in the middle of the cafeteria when no one else would. "I don't think you should invite her," Amber said as she flipped through an Essence magazine on my bed. "Why not?" I asked.
"Because the last time she was here, you tried to commit suicide."

- depression

Porsha M. Allen

THE UNWANTED WOMAN

Porsha M. Allen

You place roses on the bed,

some full with thorns,

and light incense that smells of old spice.

I have become the ritual you

practice every Sunday,

but soon you will find something more

to call your god.

- idols

What Happens In The Dark

You press your body into hers,
trying to find the place where you fit.
You swallow her earlobe with your mouth
and groan roughly in her ear.

It is dark, so you do not notice the
trail of liquid and the water damaged
mattress.

She is apologizing to God.
You press forward, interrupting
her prayers. Your fingers dent
her thighs as your eyes roll to
the back of your head.

The demons release you
from their grip as you collapse
next to her.
They have now entered
her body. Her back forms the shape
of a 'U,' and you mistake such possession
for orgasms. Her eyes find the ceiling.
She rises from the bed and flees into

the night, trying to find
someone holy enough
to cast you out.

When you kiss her slow and

realize passion doesn't live inside her,

you will roll on your back and remember me.

You will trace your fingers over all of my favorite

places and feel that my prints

are still engraved in your skin.

There,

to remind you that no one can touch you like I can.

- regret

I caught your lies with my mouth
and they didn't taste all that bad.

- acceptance

Unrequited Love

Way too many times I have watched you be human,
flawed, not fit for this world,
but I found my place in you,
right beneath your skin.

After asking you how do you like your eggs,
and fixing your plate before mine,
I realized I depended upon your presence
just a little bit more than I depended on God's.

I watch you sip coffee from my favorite mug,
and wonder if I am special enough to sip from yours.

I had not been on the inside of your apartment,
but you knew what my insides felt like.

I don't know your middle name
or what you dream about at night, but I pray it's me.
I sit down at the table across from you,
and trace your right index finger with my thumb nail.
To my surprise you don't flinch or pull away,
instead you grab my hand and lead me to your lap,
kiss my forehead and ask for more eggs.

I know that I would be foolish to move at your
command,
but there is something about your voice,
the way each word melts at the center of your tongue.
I know that you are the kind of man who knows
not what it means to love a woman,
but only how to make her love you.

But I do not complain,
submission is better than lonely.
I make your eggs just the way you like them,
scrambled with cheese, with a dash of salt and
pepper.

I knew we would not last and
that I couldn't change into your last name;
the clothes do not complement my figure.
I lay down with you one last night,
and wonder what my soulmate had planned that
evening.

I wonder how he likes his eggs;
scrambled with cheese,
with a dash of salt and pepper?

Or maybe, he doesn't like eggs at all.
Not everyone does.

I have carried the moon on my back
for men who didn't even love me enough
to tell their hearts my name.

- never enough

"Here," I said.
"Take my body,
you don't have
to give it back."

- low self-esteem

Moonlight In Vermont

There is an old record player on the Cherrywood
dresser next to the window. "Body and Soul" by
Billie Holiday floats over our heads.
There is a glow coming from your lips,
your eyes have become the place where I look for
stars.

The words, "I love you," run smoothly from my lips
as Billie sings "Moonlight in Vermont,"
her voice filling the room as the
vanilla scented candle wax melts
onto the table. The palm of your
hand greets my rising cheek.
The room is quiet and I see your chest cave in.
You exhale - heavily.
Silence holds the truth in its mouth.
I turn over and stare into the direction
of the candle.
The wax is melting slowly down its body.
I stand and move
slowly towards the door.
I stop and look down at the floor boards
and the chipping paint.

"It's just that, I am bored with how you look," you said.

I am guilty,

of laying my identity at the feet of men,

when they have done nothing

but use them to walk away.

- every time

He looked too much like the sun
   to be filled with so much darkness.

- deception

Your throat is filled with broken promises.

Each soft word that escapes your mouth knows that it

does not belong there.

But by the way you said my name,

I believed that you had a tongue worth trusting.

- but you didn't

"Are you still angry with the man who
violated you?"
asked my therapist.

"No," I said.

"I am angry with my father
for not being there to protect me."

In The Belly

It is around noon
and my mother is on her fifth beer.
Cigarette smoke whispers prayers to the wall
and my mouth is closed,
tight eyes close even tighter.

My mother birthed four children,
all housed in the marrow of her bones.
Her body knew ours before we did.
I listen as the sound of poison
travels down her throat.
The ache in my stomach tells me
that it has found hers.

I want to tell her about the moon,
and about how it gathers for prayer
with the stars and prays for her,

about how her children all pray
for her.

Mama has been crying soft tears
for years. I could hear from

inside of her womb. I kicked at her

belly to tickle the sorrow away.

I could hear her heart -

restless.

I tried to whisper to it a few

times in a different tongue,

but I was too far away.

I learned sadness from the womb.

It grew strong inside us both.

It came with my blood,

it came with my lungs,

I came out of my mother

feet first, trying to escape it –

before it killed us both.

If I am found laughing,
please, do not mistake it for
happiness. I am trying
to force the sadness to leave.

- everyday

Journal Entry
April 5, 2016

I was five when the first and only picture with my
father was taken. I was wearing a yellow jumpsuit
with a white shirt underneath. You cannot see our
teeth. His arm is placed lightly around me; maybe
so it won't take much to let go once my
mother snaps the photo, or maybe it's because he had
never done it before.
"Your daddy never held you as a baby,"
my godmother said one day when she came to visit
my mother. "Your mom gave you to him one day and
he just put you on the couch and walked away," she
said, now eating a bowl of ice cream. And I thought
to myself, *What kind of mess is that?*
"But you look just like him."

When I was twenty-one, my father approached me at
a bus stop and asked if I needed a ride home. I looked
at him, squinted my eyes,
and thought that the cars passing by probably thought
that he was a stranger. "No thank you," I said as I
saw the bus approach me. "Okay," he responded
while shrugging his shoulders. He reached out his

arm to hug me. I stepped away from the space that
now held him in it, and shook my head. I thought
about what my godmother had said just a few years
earlier, about the picture that was taken when I was
five, with his arm
loosely wrapped around me, making it easy to let go.
And I knew, the only reason why he held me for all
of 30 seconds, was because my mother asked him to.

I was an orphan
trying to find a home
in the arms of men,
but just like my father,
they decided that
they didn't want me
either.

- neglect

My body cannot lie;
I am not completely happy,
I am not completely healed.

- the truth

The Way My Mother Loves

My brother came through my mother's
front door with a knot on his head the size a grape.
The neighbor boys had tied him and his friends to a
tree again. I could tell by the deep lines in his wrists.
My mother grabbed her tennis shoes from the closet
and sweatpants from her dresser drawer. My brother
was my mama's only boy, so she had a special place
in her soul for him.
I knew her love for me was different as well for two
reasons:

1.   Because I was the youngest and
2.   Because I was only 1 pound, and the only
     child that the doctors had to cut her open to
     get to.

That explains our relationship; uneasy, difficult, and
hard on the bones.
My mother's love does not look like the love my
great-grandmother and grandmother had. For her,
love looks like stuffing money into our pockets that
she got her from her boyfriend. It's working double
shifts at the nursing homes, just so your children
won't have to hear you say, "No." It's telling your

children that you don't like them, but you love them
anyway. It is anything but soft, anything but
affectionate. It is loud. It is pulling out sweatpants
and putting on tennis shoes, charging up the street at
7 p.m. asking all of the neighborhood boys,
"Who touched my son?"

How did I not know
that you would one day leave?
Betrayal has kissed even the face
of God.

- i should have known

Some people will sense
your vulnerability and try
to devour you.

- be cautious

I visit my grandmother's grave

whenever I crave affection.

It's funny how the dead can wrap

themselves around you better than the living can.

My soul knew no harm,
until it became one with yours.

- the mistake

Cutter

I started cutting at the age of 14, the night after I had
been molested, and just weeks after watching my
grandmother return to the earth.
I didn't know any other way to *open* up.
I had nightmares about his hands, the way they
trailed over my body. I dreamed about my
grandmother reaching out to hug me, the same way
she did the last time I saw her alive.
The light-colored lines carved in my skin are all a
story, chapter by chapter, page by page, the only way
I knew how to tell it.

Porsha M. Allen

BECOMING
AND
UN-BECOMING

Her veins are still filled with last night's Moscato.
She has become all too familiar with the ceiling,
trying to conjure up all the ways to tell her body she
is sorry. She bleeds, grateful that Mother Nature
knows when to show up. She is being cleansed, of all
the men who placed themselves inside her. Their
spirits leave her body and her spirit wrestles with the
empty space trying to find comfort in lonely. But she
likes it this way; her body is learning what it is like
not to be owned, penetrated, or used. Her body is
hers, and she belongs to herself.

<u>Healing</u>

For me, healing looks
like getting up at 3 in the morning and
writing letters to God, staying up late to write poems
when I feel that ache again, or when I am feeling
lonely again.

It's apologizing to myself,
until my own actions show that I mean it.

It's not letting people tell me who they want me to
be, or what they want me to do.

It looks like broken glass on the bathroom's blue tile
floor, and my sister bursting in on me right before I
decide not to do it.

It looks like tearing my whole room apart while
screaming, hoping that everyone can hear me. It's
asking God for forgiveness.

It's forgiving my exes when they tell me they are
sorry, but never speaking to them again because there
is no reason to.

It's about being able to look my father in the eye
without feeling rage swell up in my belly.
It's wishing that my mother was someone else, but
telling her that I love her anyway.

It's forgiving myself for the things that cannot be
changed and loving myself even when the voice
inside of me tells me why I shouldn't.

Never give your heart to someone
who hasn't first given theirs to God.

- i have learned the hard way

This blood may not be holy enough to
sip during communion,
but it will be good enough for me.
It will be good enough to stand in, live in,
be in, and move in.
It is good enough,
I am good enough.

Never lose your ability to smile,
for you will need it on the days
you feel like falling apart,
but can't.

- be strong

I have learned to never place
my happiness in the hands of humans;
they are not my savior,
their spine wasn't made
strong enough to bare such responsibility.

- save yourself

On the day she gets to heaven,
she will dip her feet in the sea
of forgetfulness and be reminded
of all the times that her sins were
forgiven.

I drained myself of you today
and suddenly I began to float,
with ease, so beautifully.

- free

I forgive myself, for all the sins
that I have committed for the sake
of love.
I forgive myself...
I forgive myself...
I forgive myself...

Wholeness

I am standing in the middle of a field,
with my skin baking in the sun.
I am melting the anger away.
The ground is filled with plants all asking for water.
My feet are facing wild flowers and the seeds planted
in my stomach are sprouting up my spine.
I raise my fingers toward the sky and push.
I press into it. I can feel the wind lifting me off the
ground. I am growing to love myself as I answer to
nature's voice and search for God in the clouds.
I rest my head onto the grass, scattered throughout
the earth, running my fingers through freedom,
tasting the land and all of its glory.
I am changing,
I am growing,
I am learning
what it takes
to become whole.

Porsha M. Allen

<u>FLY</u>

I lit the candles and ushered you in closer,
my body had grown accustomed to your touch.
You meet me in my bedroom as I close the door
behind us,
you always knew where to look for me.
I hide between sadness and the belly of lonely,
I hear its stomach growl.
It's been weeks since it has tasted my skin.

But I have not completely known happiness;
I search for the meaning of it in your laughter,
and in the way you dance on your toes in the
middle of my bedroom floor.
Maybe it's tucked away in your heart,
too stubborn and unwilling to allow me in
to feel what it is like to live freely.
Come here my love, and let me suck the smile from
your lips.
I don't have one of my own, may I please borrow
yours?

And what about your limbs?
You move so carelessly, reminding me of clouds

when they sweep away the moon.
I know you are happy, and I have not yet known such
a thing,
but I can see it in your eyes.
They remind me of the rainbows
that burst from the sky after a storm.
They are the only thing that put me to sleep at night.
It is not your body that I crave,
it is the light hidden beneath your skin.
It shines in the morning, drags me out of bed,
and melts layers of sorrow from my bones.

You told me to gather up all of my possessions
and store them in your bosom.
I cried on your chest that night,
and I felt your warmth.
You were glowing from the inside out,
I could hardly stand it.
A blue jay flew across an oak tree
and rested its wings on my windowsill.
I swore I saw it smile in your direction.
It tapped the window with its beak
and you ushered him in.
I lit another candle, we both needed
to heal and gain the strength to fly.

Tonight had nothing to do with lust,

tonight was more than flesh.

Ashes trailed down my cheeks.

As a child, my temple had been burned down,

and your arms were the altar in

which I laid down my burdens.

Tonight started with a kiss,

but would end with eternal wings.

If someone hurts you,

forgive them

in order to regain your power,

and be able to give yourself completely to God.

For it is then that your love is sure

to be reciprocated beyond measure.

Life has taught me that making a mistake
is a part of human nature,
but learning from it and using it as an opportunity
to grow is a part of character.

- *growth*

Listen to your body and stop
fighting for someone who isn't
worth such a war.

- you are losing

<u>Her</u>

If I should have a daughter,
I would bathe her in purity and clothe her in self-
respect. I would trace the life lines in her palms back
to her roots and tell her she is strong. I will pray with
her and whisper scriptures in her ear, so that God's
word would come flowing out of her bloodstream. I'd
gather up everything I was ever taught about being a
woman, find the pieces that were missing from my
soul, and store them in her chest. She would breathe
much differently. Her soul wouldn't reek of regret
and she would smell much sweeter. I pray that she
never learns pain the way that I have, and never
discovers that he does not love her until it is too late.
I will show her what it means to have arms, and that
love is something she should never have to beg for.
She will know her place in the world, and unwrap
galaxies from her hair. She will learn how to make
tea with just enough sugar and lemon juice. I will tell
her that her great-grandmother loved to decorate and
sew and that as a child, I picked blue and black
berries from trees and watched her great-great-
grandmother bake pies from scratch. She will know
all of these things and what it means to love herself.

Be the person who fights for you.

When someone lies to you,
they are telling you that you
are not worthy of the truth.

- but you are

I am finally learning to make peace
with all of my imperfections.

- after all these years

Promise me something;
promise me that you will be
everything they said you couldn't.

There is both good and bad in the world.
Be the bit of beauty left in the world.
Be the bit of God left in the world.

I close my eyes and think about the earth.
I see my blood returning back to the ground as I
watch the roots of a tree swallow its thickness.
I am reminded of how to breathe, how to let go of the
pain. I am giving myself new reasons to bleed, to
make room for all that is beautiful.

If you crawled into my past,
you would not look the same when you came out.

- what tragedies will do

I wonder how many times my own
body cried out to me whenever I
welcomed someone so unworthy of it.

- i apologize

There is too much blood in this body,

so I call on my veins to relinquish it.

Even our blood wants a little bit of freedom to know

what it is like to live outside of the body;

that is why it is always a bit messy when it leaves us.

- always

You will never need anyone
more than you need yourself.

- as it should be

I am thankful for those

who have given me wounds,

they have given me much to write about,

giving me a place

to put my tears.

- grateful

Porsha M. Allen

There is a glow hidden in your chest.
This tells me that you are not the darkness
they made you out to be.
You are not what they call bad.

- don't listen to them

I have found God in my skin
and magic in my bones.
I have used my aches and pains
to soil the ground, and grow into who
I have always wished to be.

- evolving

You are not lost,
for you know where you can be found.

- rediscovering

Porsha M. Allen

I am grateful for the gravity of grace
by which God has used to uphold me.
Without it, I would be nothing more
than a fallen star.

87

I have learned that addictions
are simply escape mechanisms gone wrong.

- sadly

Give yourself the thing you feel most unworthy of.

(For me, that would look a lot like love.)

I am a burning building,
and the only body of water
that can save me.

- survival

The End

Porsha M. Allen

About the author

Porsha M. Allen is a 22-year-old poet and writer from Richmond, Virginia. At the age of 9, Porsha discovered her passion for writing when her grandmother gave her a journal. Since then, Porsha has been dedicated to her craft with the hopes that it will heal those who read her work. In being fatherless, heartbroken, and abused, Porsha used writing as a way to heal and now helps others do the same. Porsha earned her Bachelor's Degree in English from the Virginia Union University, and plans to continue her education at Queens University of Charlotte where she will study poetry.

About the book

How She Bleeds is a body of work filled with emotion, trauma, heartache and abandonment, while one's own strength is realized in the aftermath. This book speaks about the horrors of sexual abuse, the pain of unrequited love, and having the strength to endure hardships. Her words are both haunting and healing, taking the reader on a journey through the most heartbreaking and life changing moments of the writer's life. This work of raw honesty and vulnerability will undoubtedly leave the reader longing for more.

CPSIA information can be obtained
at www.ICGtesting.com
Printed in the USA
BVHW03s2158240618
519940BV00001B/70/P